BARTHOLOMEW ROBERTS' MERCY

JEREMY MCLEAN

POINTS OF SAIL
PUBLISHING

Points of Sail Publishing
P.O. Box 30083 Prospect Plaza
FREDERICTON, New Brunswick
E3B 0H8, Canada

Edited by Ethan James Clarke
http://silverjay-editing.com/

This is a work of fiction. Any similarity to persons, living or dead, is purely coincidental… Or is it?

ACKNOWLEDGEMENTS

Thanks to all my friends and family for helping me.
This wouldn't have been written if not for their support.

And thank you to you, reader. You make the story come alive
with your imagination, and without you these words are just
ink on a page.

TABLE OF CONTENTS

1. THE TRIAL

From the Journal of Bartholomew Roberts
Entry #54 Dated July 5th, No Year Given

We sail for Providencia with a brief stop in San Andrés for re-supply.

I find myself on the eve of a years- long journey to find Walter Kennedy, the Irishman who stole my ship. Though our fates are set to intertwine once more, it brings me no pleasure.

There will be a battle ahead, and a decision I must make.

We have enlisted the aid of Edward Thatch, better known as the upstart pirate Blackbeard, in the battle to come. He is presently delayed due to an unfortunate meeting with a Spanish Galleon. He bid me to continue on as he made repairs to his ship, offering spare crewmates to hasten our voyage, and promised to meet again in Providencia.

He asked me what I would do to Kennedy upon meeting with him once more, to which I said I would deliver God's justice. He stated that if he met with the one he wanted revenge on, he would kill the man. I pondered aloud whether that was a just action that God would approve of, and he said that it was a pirate's justice.

Can the two not be the same?

Fortune anchored in the harbour of San Andrés. A small English colony had been built into the northeast of the island and taken over the paradise. Many of the tropical trees and wildlife which would have spread to the edge of the island had been cut back for wooden homes and buildings across the shore. A few larger brick buildings dotted the northern side and interior of the island.

"Hank, I'm going ashore for a time. Would you handle the re-supply for us?"

Hank nodded as he placed his thumbs between his belt and trousers. "You can count on me, Captain."

"Good man," Roberts replied with a smack against Hank's back.

"What will you be doing in town?"

"There's a chance the pirates we're after stopped by here on their way to Providencia. No harm in asking around to see if any of the townsfolk saw their ships."

After Hank nodded again, Roberts turned around and headed to the quarterdeck ladder towards the longboats. "We'll get him," Hank said behind him.

Roberts looked over his shoulder at Hank. His eyes were wide and there was a smirk curling the corner of his lips. "Of course," Roberts replied. He had to force himself to return the smile, and his muscles pulled against the change in expression.

After three days of hard labour, working day and night

to reach San Andrés in time, Roberts had had no time alone to think. Going ashore would be as much about information gathering as it would be to contemplate what he would do when he met Walter Kennedy again.

Roberts boarded one of the longboats bound for shore to return supplies to the *Fortune*. The men aboard were talking excitedly about the upcoming battle, and their soon-to-be revenge.

That's right, these men must also feel betrayed by Kennedy and their old crewmates.

The longboat, powered by strong rowers, was soon docked at the pier of San Andrés, and the *Fortune's* other longboats were not far behind.

The sounds of the pier overwhelmed all other noises. Men were shouting, rolling barrels, dropping boxes, and stamping their feet at the bustling though small pier. Roberts once more found no respite, and couldn't focus on his thoughts amidst the noise.

He left the longboat as his men were lashing it to the wooden pier and walked into town. He barely took notice of the sights around him, but what he did see was the same stale colony life followed by many from Britain. Dull wooden houses, horses pulling carts over cobbled stone or dirt, dainty women in dresses and men of various garb according to their station, and mud. Always mud.

Roberts soon found himself in a tavern, devoid of most patrons, and he sat himself at a table in the corner of the room. Soon, a young woman asked him what he wanted, and went to fetch him a meal and some ale.

Out a window, Roberts could see the sun descending on the town in a slow arc. It was nearing time for an evening sup, but would still be a few hours before night-fall.

Should Hank haste in re-supplying the ship, we could arrive in Providencia in the middle of the night.

The young woman returned with a mug filled to the brim with a pale ale in one hand, and a plate lined with several cured meats, soft cheeses, and biscuits in the other.

"My thanks, my dear," Roberts said. He cocked his head to the side as he gazed into the young woman's hazel eyes. "Tell me, would you happen to know if any frigates happened upon your shores of late? Tall ships outfitted for battle?" Roberts asked, gesturing with his hands.

The young woman smiled, but seemed flustered at the inquiry. She looked off to the side in thought. "Well, sir, we see several merchants in these parts… and pirates, if that's your meaning."

Roberts cocked his brow. "Pirates?" he asked, not knowing much of the colony.

The girl nodded and held her arms close to her chest, as if warmth had escaped her in that brief moment. "Yes sir, pirates," she replied. "They attack on occasion, but never in earnest. A few merchants lose their cargo before they can be chased off, nothing more."

"Have there been any recent attacks?"

"Umm, yes, actually. There was one a few weeks ago. The pirates left empty-handed though, and one of them was captured."

"Their luck left them that day, wouldn't you say?" Roberts said with a smirk before taking a long drink of his ale.

The girl smiled along with him for a moment. "Are you staying in town for the afternoon, sir?"

Roberts nodded. "I will be here until nightfall."

"Should you like it, the pirate is on trial right now at the courthouse in the centre of town."

Roberts' ears perked up. "Oh? Is that why it's so empty here?" he said, looking around at the empty chairs and stools, and clean tables.

The girl nodded. "It's not so often we have a pirate on trial," she said, dimples showing at the corners of her cheeks. "If you want to see it, it's in a large brick building, you can't miss it."

"My thanks for the ale, the food, the information, and most of all your pretty smile," Roberts said as he too smiled and placed a coin in her hand.

The girl blushed bright red and thanked Roberts before heading back to the other side of the tavern.

Roberts took a slice of the marbled meat and a piece of sharp cheddar together and placed it on the edge of one of the biscuits, then took a bite. He looked out the window to the blue-yellow sky as the three different textures and tastes mixed to create a sublime taste greater than the sum of its parts.

A pirate's trial, hmm?

Roberts ate a few more slices of meat, a few more pieces of cheese, and another biscuit before chugging the large mug of pale ale. After he finished he set the mug down with a boisterous sigh, and then rose from his seat.

Roberts tossed the girl another coin on his way to the front of the tavern before exiting the establishment. He headed towards the centre of the town, searching for the courthouse the girl mentioned.

He walked up the muddy cobblestone, slick with water from rain or lingering puddles, and when he reached his destination it was just as the girl had said: there was no missing the courthouse.

Bartholomew Roberts' Justice

The large brick building was longer and slightly taller than any other building around, and men and women of all ages were spilling out of its confines. The double doors at the front were wide open; not that it mattered though, as people had crowded around and blocked the way inside and all the way to the bottom of the stairs leading up. On the sides of the building, children and adults alike were standing atop boxes and barrels trying to catch a glimpse inside through the windows. More people were talking in groups and hovering around the stairs and entrance, not wanting to get involved with the larger crowd and bustle, but still interested in the goings on inside.

Ah, to lead a colony life such as this, where the most excitement is the trial of a pirate. Roberts let out a short laugh at the thought, then made his way up to the entrance.

As he passed by the townsfolk, he could hear them talking of the trial and what was going on inside. Each spoke of the villainy and the unspeakable atrocities the accused committed, and each person's recollection was more sinister than the last.

Roberts pushed past the men and women crowded around the entrance. As he tried to squeeze his large frame through the throng many flashed him dirty looks followed by wary glances. Soon, the commotion his well-above-average height caused forced others to look his way and move aside before he got near. A small part in the sea of the crowd formed, and they ushered him further into the courthouse.

Inside the courthouse, the waning light of the day provided a slight amount of light. The whole building was open, with a tall ceiling, and a large gallery for people to watch in the middle and the sides.

Near the entrance was an elevated wooden platform with two armed men blocking the stairs up. A man stood atop the podium, but Roberts wasn't able to see his face. Judging from the way he was wringing the life out of the cap in his hands, Roberts knew the man was in distress. A mirror reflected the little light from the windows straight on the man, so all could watch him with ease.

On the other end of the courtroom, another, taller podium took up much of the far wall. There sat five men wearing powdered wigs and ornate outfits of black and gold. Roberts could only assume, by their position, appearance, and sour disposition, that they were a panel of judges overseeing the trial.

Throughout the ordeal of entering and finding a suitable spot from which to listen and watch, Roberts caught the gist of the trial. From what he could gather, they were nearing the end, but it seemed like it had been drawn out for some time. Witnesses had been called, and a neutral party was recapping the pirate's various murders and depravities for the court.

Roberts found a spot in the gallery where he could see both the judges and the accused with ease. Looking at the pirate, he was a sorry sight. He had been washed for the trial, but fresh wounds covered his head, neck, and hands. Dark spots from punches or kicks had turned his skin a sickly colour, and his face took on a ghostly pallor from weakness and malnourishment. Even had he been well fed, the look in his eyes did not show Roberts he was a battle-hardened pirate. Either the man was a coward, or things were not as they seemed.

"Does the accused have any final words before deliberation?" the judge in the centre asked.

There was a small pause, and then the pirate spoke up.

Bartholomew Roberts' Justice

"Sirs, I say again that I am no pirate. I am falsely accus—"

The head judge held up his hand to silence the pirate. The judges looked perturbed, and the townsfolk in the gallery shouted and booed. The head judge called for silence, and soon the crowd quieted.

"The only falsehood… is the one you have been spouting here. We have brought witnesses forth to speak of your barbarisms. Give yourself some lasting grace, and admit your crimes."

The accused was on the verge of tears, and his fingers went white against the cap in his hands. "Please, you must listen to—"

"Enough," the judge shouted. "It is clear that you do not repent your actions in the least." The judge glanced to his contemporaries, and they nodded back at him. "This court finds you guilty of piracy, indecency, and acts of violence and depravity against the citizens of this fine town. By our powers given by the grace of God, and these citizens, you are hereby sentenced to death by hanging," the judge announced to raucous cheers.

As the town threw shame upon the man, Roberts couldn't help but become angered. Looking at the sorry state he was in, the words he said, and his own experience working with the world's best liars, cheats, and killers, he could tell that the man wasn't lying. He was no pirate, and he was about to hang for a crime he didn't commit.

This is not God's justice, only man's.

"Sentence will commence at sunset," the judge said. "This court is now dismissed."

Roberts found himself heading towards the exit of the courthouse without thought. He pushed past the others trying to leave the gallery and watched as guards took the accused away in chains. The guards took him outside of the courthouse, and Roberts followed close behind.

Upon exiting, the crowd threw all manner of things at the accused, from small rocks to vegetables. Though he suspected none truly knew the man or witnessed his crimes, they were willing to part with expensive vegetables that had taken so long to cultivate. Even if the accusations had been true, it spoke of the hatred those men and women held in their hearts in that moment.

Walking over the broken and smashed vegetables, Roberts continued to follow the trio at a distance. Other citizens followed as well, continuing to throw insults and objects at the man. As they ran out of items or patience, the other people began to trickle away and stop following, but Roberts continued onward.

Roberts wasn't sure himself why he kept following the man, but an idea soon formed in his head. *When I have the chance, I'll help him escape.*

Roberts waited, watching the three for a moment of opportunity. Out of the range of the angry voices, Roberts could hear the heavy plop of footsteps splashing water from crevices in the stone, and the piercing clang of the chains dangling off the man's listless arms and dragging legs.

The guards turned in front of a building, and the accused stopped in his tracks. He pulled his head up, and Roberts could swear he heard a large crick from the wrenching of unused bones. A few seconds passed with him standing there, deathly still, a painting of what was soon to come etched into Robert's memories.

Now! It must be now!

Before Roberts could act, the accused shoved his elbow into one of the guards, toppling him over to the wet stones below. He bent down and jumped over the guard before the other one could react, and ran as best he could down an alley.

The second guard shouted at the accused and ran after him down the alley as the first guard picked himself off the ground to give chase.

The man's escape attempt shocked Roberts still for a moment, but he ran after the three when he regained his composure. Halfway down the alley, the accused was lying on the ground, huddled up as one of the guards kicked him in the stomach. The other guard, the one who was attacked, bent over and clutched his chest to catch his breath.

"He's a feisty one," Roberts commented.

The two guards looked at him for a second, taking note of his size, but the escape attempt suppressed their awe. "Aye, but we caught the bastard," the uninjured guard said before he went back to kicking the man on the ground.

Roberts walked closer to the injured guard, and just as he reared back his massive fist the man's expression twisted. Roberts slammed his fist into the man's jaw, and his face smashed on the stone, splashing more water and mud over the surrounding rocks.

The noise drew the second guard's attention, but before he could react Roberts grabbed him by the face and lifted him off the ground. He threw the man into the wall of the building beside him, slamming his back against the brick. Roberts let go, and the man fell in a heap.

Roberts bent down and searched the guards' belongings for a key. After fumbling through pockets and belts, he found a set of keys on an iron loop, and rose to his feet.

Roberts looked over at the man accused of piracy. His

mouth was agape and his breathing heavy. Sweat dripped down his cheeks and over the bruises and scars on his face.

"Wh— who are you?" he asked. "What do you want with me?"

Roberts walked over, and the man tried to back away. "It's alright, friend. I'm here to save you."

The man calmed as Roberts reached over and used the keys on his shackles. "Why are you helping me?"

Roberts tried each of the keys on the loop, none of them working. "I was at your trial, and over the years I've learned how to tell when someone is telling the truth. You are no pirate, and I could not let this injustice stand." After a moment, Roberts found the correct key and unshackled the man.

Roberts helped the man to his shaking feet, who then dusted himself off. He held his hand out to Roberts. "I am called Desmond," he said.

Roberts shook the man's hand with a firm grip. "I am Bartholomew Roberts. It is a pleasure to meet you, Desmond."

Desmond's brow raised at Roberts' name. He looked away, his focus elsewhere. "Bartholomew Roberts… where have I heard that name?"

Roberts laughed, his hefty chest heaving with each bellow. "Perhaps you've heard of the pirate, Bartholomew Roberts?" he offered.

Desmond's eyes widened. "Ah yes, that must be it…" He stared at Roberts for a moment, and Roberts held a grin on his face as he watched his expression change. "D—Don't tell me… you're…?" he said with a shaky point of the finger.

Roberts nodded. "I am the pirate Bartholomew Roberts," he confirmed.

Desmond stepped back from Roberts, his eyes as wide as saucers and his brows upturned like the arched back of a cat. "W-what do you want with me? You know I'm not a pirate… stay back!" he said at once, his hands raised in front of him.

Roberts held his hands up. "Desmond, as I told you, I came to help you. I know you're not a pirate, but I can help you escape from here. My ship is bound for Providencia. Upon arrival you are free to leave, but any further stay here would be… unwise," he said. Desmond still looked wary, but his legs had firmed up, and his hands returned to his sides. Roberts folded his arms and let out a sigh. "You have two options: come with me if you want to live, or stay here and perish."

Desmond stared at Roberts for another moment, and his eyes slowly lost the fear they had once had. "I want to go with you."

"Good choice," Roberts said with a smirk. He walked over and pulled Desmond further down the alley. "It would be best if we avoided the main streets for now."

Roberts and Desmond went down the alley and around the bend behind another house, then headed towards the harbour where the *Fortune* waited. They were careful to check each alley for people before walking down one, and alternated between the different streets when no one was looking.

"So, what brought you such misfortune, friend?" Roberts asked as he looked around the corner of a wooden house.

"Truly, I don't know who it was I angered," he replied. "I'm a sailor, nothing more. I don't belong with any company, and so I find work on the next port. The night before the true villains attacked, I had far too much to drink, and I found myself in the tank the following morning." The two men moved down the next street. "No sooner had I awoken than I was charged with piracy."

"Tch," Roberts spat. "They meant for you to serve as scapegoat for the attack to appease the populace."

"That looks the size of it."

"Well, no more, friend. Look, there is our longboat. We make it to that, and we are free." Roberts pointed to the longboats they had used to arrive at the pier. His men were loading them with supplies of barrels, bags, and boxes. "And we seem to have fortune on our side; my men are about to set off. Come, your freedom awaits," Roberts said, looking over his shoulder with a grin pulling at his cheeks.

Before they could make for the pier, they heard loud shouting coming from the centre of town. Both of their heads snapped to the side, towards the noise, and their expressions grew dire.

"We must move, now," Roberts said.

"Yes."

Roberts went out from the house they were hiding behind and walked at a brisk but leisurely pace towards the pier. Desmond came up beside him, kept his head down, and tried to hide behind the side of the larger man.

As they walked they passed by some villagers, but the men and women were too busy looking at the commotion towards the centre of town to take notice. Their pace quickened the closer they were to the pier, and soon their boots were slamming on the wooden planks as they ran to the longboats.

"Men, we have a new recruit, and it is imperative that he returns to *Fortune* post-haste."

Bartholomew Roberts' Justice

Roberts pulled Desmond over to one of the longboats already filled with cargo. Desmond climbed inside, aided, or hindered, by Roberts' insistent pushing and prodding.

Every few seconds Roberts glanced from Desmond and the longboat over to the pier where they had come from. His head and eyes darted back and forth across the wooden platform as he searched for trouble.

After Desmond sat in the longboat and Roberts began entering it, trouble came. Several men from the local militia stormed out of town to the pier. One man at the head of the pack looked back and forth down the pier, then waved his hand to those with him. The men spread out down the pier and began questioning the merchants and fishermen there.

"Get down, get down!" Roberts ordered in a loud whisper as he waved his hand towards Desmond.

Desmond dropped from his seat and went under the plank, lying flat against the bottom of the longboat. "W-what should I do?" Desmond stuttered, the tremor inside escaping him as he spoke.

"Stay still, and don't make a sound," Roberts said. He looked over to his men. "Men, as you were."

Roberts glanced around the longboat, then reached over and grabbed a rolled blanket from the side. He unfurled it and threw it on top of the plank and covered Desmond. Roberts touched up the edges of the blanket to cover the man fully, then sat down in the longboat.

As soon as he sat down, one of the armed militiamen walked over to them. "Have any of you noticed a man of your build with bruises pass by here recently?" he asked.

Roberts' men shook their heads. "Should we be concerned, sir?" Roberts asked.

The militiaman looked at Roberts, taking in his height.

14

"No, nothing a man of your stature need concern himself with." The man glanced around at the longboats Roberts' crew were filling with supplies, and the large stacks piled near the edge of the pier offshoot they were on. "What's all this?"

"Supplies for our trip. Headed north to Port Royal."

The man nodded and took a few steps around the supplies, looking them over as he held his weapon tight. Roberts flashed his men looks, and their hands rested at their hips, close to their hidden weapons. Roberts inched his hand over to the side of the longboat where a musket was fastened. He didn't pull it out, but kept his hand steady on the barrel.

The militiaman took his time looking over the cargo, glancing in the longboats for far longer than was necessary. His eyes were sharp, and his brows sharper still. They were furrowed down towards the bridge of his nose, wrinkles appearing in the gap.

"Is there a problem with our cargo, sir?"

"No, no issues here," the man replied. "What was it you were transporting again?"

Roberts forced a smile. "Didn't say, sir. We're bringing bibles to the new world." Roberts took his hand off the musket, reached in his pocket, and pulled out the bible he had. "Nothing more needed than the holy word for the heathen natives. Why not sit with us for a spell, and we can talk scripture?" Roberts asked, a bit of Hank's vocabulary creeping in.

The man shook his head. "No time for that, preacher," he said. "Carry on."

The militiaman nodded to the group of them, and then moved on down the pier to continue his search. After the sound of his boots smacking against the wood was far enough away, Roberts let out a sigh. Beneath him, he could hear Desmond mimicking him.

Roberts lifted the edge of the blanket to see Desmond there, looking up at him. "Just a bit longer and we'll be on our ship," Roberts said.

Desmond nodded. "You sure are quick-footed. If I didn't know any better, I'd believe your story too."

Roberts bowed. "My thanks," he said before laughing.

Roberts placed the blanket down, then brought out oars. His crewmates released the longboat from the dock, and Roberts rowed the boat back to the *Fortune*. Once there, Roberts and Desmond climbed up rope ladders to board as other crewmates prepared to bring up the longboat full of supplies.

Hank met with Roberts and Desmond. "Welcome back, Captain," he said. "Another stowaway for us?"

"Yes, it appears that way. Desmond, this is my first mate, Hank Abbott. Hank, this is Desmond. He was falsely accused of piracy, so I thought to help him reach safe haven in Providencia."

Hank grinned as he nodded. "I understand. So, am I to assume we should prepare to leave?"

"As soon as the supplies are aboard, yes. The sooner the better."

Hank nodded once more, then looked at Desmond. "Pleasure meeting you Desmond," he said.

Desmond returned the pleasantry, and Hank headed back to the helm to instruct the crew. "Sir, I cannot thank you enough for the kindness you have shown me this day. I—"

Roberts placed both his hands on the man's shoulders. "I will have no more talk of giving thanks. I only did what righteousness demanded."

Desmond grinned. "For a pirate to talk of righteousness… the world is surely in a sorry state," he said.

Roberts nodded and stroked his chin. "Yes, that it is. We do all that we can to simply live another day it seems."

"By your mercy, and the Lord's grace, I shall see another. I only hope that tomorrow's trial is not so difficult to overcome as this one."

"That is every man's hope," Roberts replied. He smirked. "Now, what say we have a toast to celebrate your head remaining on your shoulders?"

Desmond gave a morbid chuckle. "That sounds delightful."

2. SABOTAGE

From the Journal of Bartholomew Roberts
Entry #56 Dated July 7th, No Year Given

A young man named Desmond has temporarily joined our outfit for the short trip between San Andrés and Providencia.

He was to be hanged for supposed crimes, though he claimed innocence. Believing in that innocence, I took it upon myself to free the man from his bondage and eventual undue punishment.

Am I a fool to act thusly? Each action as a pirate brings with it a bevy of possible consequences, and any action that brings attention to us can bring no good.

And yet, to stand idly by would mean I would be as much to blame for the man's death as those who falsely convicted him.

When is it just to let someone die, or for that matter, to kill? The bible says thou shalt not kill, but also to follow the laws of man as they are there by the will of God.

But, if all men sin, how can man's laws be without sin?

Fortune arrived at Providencia well after nightfall, when the moon and the stars were all that illuminated their journey. The star's reflection danced on the waves in their path and wake.

From the little light available it was hard to see the town properly, but the ships in the harbour and the homes and businesses were lit up from lanterns. A lighthouse to the east of the harbour shone its light down their way, and helped the crew of *Fortune* anchor far away from the other tallships.

To avoid detection, Roberts also had the crew cover the name of their ship with loose canvas. It gave the appearance of a ramshackle ship, but protected them from the crews that knew the name.

Once anchored, Roberts made to join some crewmates ashore to look for Walter Kennedy and his crew. It was late into night, but not so late that night-time revelry was at an end. Roberts hoped that they would find Kennedy and his comrades amongst the revellers.

Roberts and Hank boarded a longboat for shore with ten other crewmates and their fugitive stowaway Desmond. The dark waters illuminated by a lantern swinging off the bow. The light bounced off the water and cast long shadows on the creases and wrinkles on his crew's cragged faces. Their expressions reflected the sombre tone of the time of day, and what they were about to do.

Bartholomew Roberts' Justice

"Hank, I would have you and some men inspect the taverns and inns ashore. I and the rest will see if we can find Kennedy or his companions' ships aboard this longboat."

"How will you know what ships are theirs?"

"I would not be much of a captain were I to forget the faces of my former men. Should my memory fail me, luck may be on our side if Kennedy is captain of one of the ships. I have an idea of what the name of that ship may be."

Hank nodded. "Understood, Captain. If we find anything I'll send a man out to look for you on the pier."

Desmond, sitting nearby, leaned in closer to Roberts. "Searching for someone in Providencia?" he asked.

"Yes… an old crewmate who stole away with one of our vessels some time ago."

Desmond's eyes seemed to light up like a child seeing a new toy. "That so?" he said, pulling in closer still. "You going to have some battle at sea over the ship you lost? Pirate's vengeance on the high seas?"

Roberts paused for a moment, thinking over the prospect. "I should like to avoid a battle if possible." He looked off to the side of the longboat.

"Right, right…" Desmond said, trailing off as he looked at Roberts.

Is that what we're really here for? Vengeance, not justice? Roberts took in a deep breath of the cool night air and let it out.

The longboat knocked up against the pier, and the men staying behind held it steady for those leaving. With a last goodbye, Hank left towards the town, his boots echoing off the wooden planks over the moonlit waters.

Roberts stepped up to the dock and helped Desmond

up to the pier. "Well, my friend, I suppose this is where we part ways."

"I suppose so..." Desmond replied. He put his hand out to shake Roberts'. "Though it was a short journey, I enjoyed the company of you and your men, Roberts. If only all pirates were as you were, perhaps the seas would be safer."

Roberts chuckled and shook Desmond's hand. "If only," he said.

After another pleasantry, Desmond went off towards town, leaving Roberts and his remaining crewmates at the longboat.

Roberts jumped back into the longboat, where his crew waited for him.

"So Captain, what's the plan? Douse the lantern and push the boat around the harbour?" one crewmate asked.

Roberts put palm to chin as he thought it over. He looked around at the other ships with men aboard them, drinking and singing, distracted, and then scanned the water. The stars were visible against the dark water, broken only by the waves from their boat.

"We're easily spotted on a night such as this," Roberts said. "We must blend in by standing out. How much of the good stuff do we have?"

The five crewmates who remained with Roberts checked their surroundings, under their legs and behind them, searching for bottles. A few pulled out several bottles filled with dark liquid from under their seats.

"That should do. Take us out, and get your singing voices ready men. We're celebrating."

After Roberts instructed the crew to make it look as if they were drinking to intoxication rather than actually drinking to intoxication, they rowed the longboat out towards the middle of the harbour.

Roberts motioned to the crewmates rowing to move aside and he took over. "Sing, men, sing!" he said in a forceful whisper.

The crew glanced from side to side at their mates, unsure of who would answer the call first, and nervous to be the one to start. Two of the boys stuttered and started singing, and the others joined in, sipping from their drinks between beats.

> ♪ In Amsterdam there lived a maid,
> Mark well what I do say!
> In Amsterdam there lived a maid,
> And she was mistress of her trade.
> I'll go no more a-roving with you fair maid! ♪

Roberts shifted his strokes to his mate's singing beat, keeping it slow and methodical. The sound of his strokes overpowered the men's song at first, but as they sipped on their drinks they soon found their voices.

His mates' breathing carried the smell of the alcohol to his nose, tickling it with harsh bitterness. He turned his head to the side and focused on the rowing and the smell of the sea and the song they sang.

They were quick to reach the tallships anchored in the harbour, the men aboard drinking on the weather deck in the cold night. They wore thick coats and wool caps as they drank from tin cups.

> ♪ Windy weather boys, stormy weather, boys
> When the wind blows we're all together, boys
> Blow ye winds westerly, blow ye winds, blow
> Jolly sou'wester, boys, steady she goes. ♪

Roberts weaved the boat to and fro, bringing them close enough to the tallships to read the names painted on their sides. He couldn't see any ship that he was familiar with, so he kept rowing.

As the longboat passed the ships, the crews took note of Roberts and his men and their boisterousness. The jovial singing from his crew—who had perhaps taken a bit too much to drink in the spirit of things—had roused the men on the tallships to join in. Most of the ships were near to one another, and so began a great chorus on the sea. Dozens of men began singing in unison, and their voices carried across the waters and bounced off ships' hulls. It was loud enough for Roberts to feel it in his chest.

> ♪ Gather together young men and hear this tale
> Of a man of the seas you all should know well
> His name is Great Gus and of this you be sure
> He was the best mate ye could ask for in all the land ♪

Roberts was singing along as well, to keep with their ruse. Being Welsh, Roberts had a natural singing voice, given the language's melodic nature, and he often enjoyed chanting side by side with his crew. He had to force himself to stay seated, as the chorus caused an itch in his heel. He wanted to join his men in their light dance aboard the longboat, but he needed to pay attention to the names of the ships.

There was the *Black Pearl*, the *Inferno*, the *Seaswift*, and the *Surprise* to Roberts' right, closer to the town. And to his left, further to sea, he saw the *Jack and Nab*, the *Captain's Delight*, and *At The Ready*. They varied in size and class, and some didn't even have a gun deck to speak of, which eliminated them from the possibilities.

The rowing was slow and tiring, and Roberts didn't have the luxury of a reprieve as his crewmates seemed to forget their purpose after a time. They passed ship after ship at a steady pace for nearly an hour, and Roberts couldn't see any ship name that he recognized.

Then, as the longboat passed the middle of the harbour, he saw three sloops of war anchored parallel to each other. The first had two masts, and the other two ships had three each.

When Roberts noticed the name of the first ship his singing stopped in his throat, a lump gripping hold of his voice.

The name *Gallant* was written on the side of the small sloop-of-war—the same name for a ship that his old friend-turned-enemy Walter Kennedy said he would use should he become a captain.

The other men didn't take notice of Roberts' sudden pause in the middle of their shanty, and continued to sing unawares of their Captain's demeanour. The crews of the various ships also kept up the chant, though many were now off-tempo with those who started the tune.

Roberts resumed rowing, and turned the longboat around to bring it back to the pier. He couldn't tell if it was from the constant rowing, or from seeing the name of that ship, but his heart was pounding in his ears and he felt hot around the collar. The jolly chants of his brothers turned to nothing, and all he could hear was the pounding of his chest and deep breaths through his nose.

The boat smacked against the pier and bounced back, jolting the other crewmates back to awareness. They stopped their singing short and glanced around at their surroundings. Off in the distance, the ships they had left were still singing those well-travelled tunes, and they could still be heard even at the pier.

"Captain, are you well? You look a touch flush," one of the men said.

Another man held out a bottle of rum towards Roberts. "Here, Captain, for what ails you."

Roberts glanced up at the dark bottle in front of him, then took it in hand and chugged a generous amount. He barely felt the sting as it burned his tongue and throat on the way down. He let out a loud gasp as he removed the bottle from his lips and handed it back to his crewmate.

"He's here," Roberts said. "Walter Kennedy is here, of this I have no doubt."

Some of the men's eyes widened as they glanced from Roberts back out to the many ships in the harbour. "How can you be sure? Did you see his ship?"

Roberts nodded. "Aye, the *Gallant*, the smallest in that line of ships over there," he said as he nodded towards the three sloops-of-war.

The crewmates all turned to look at the three ships Roberts motioned towards. After a quick glance, they looked at him again, this time with wide grins and devilish smiles.

"Now we jus' have to find the bastard, then we'll show him what-for, right Captain?"

Roberts looked up at the crewmate who spoke. A grin curled the corners of his lips, and his eyes betrayed a deep lust for blood and vengeance. Roberts wondered if his own eyes looked that way as well, such was his anger in that moment. He simply nodded to the crewmate, and the men turned into schoolchildren eager for a tussle.

Roberts' face was still hot, and his thoughts were on

his former friend and crewmate who wronged him. He cast his gaze to the floorboards of the longboat. *Why do I feel such anger in my heart? How long has this hate been brewing in my soul?* Roberts looked up at his jovial mates in front of him. *Is it wrong to feel this way?* Roberts sat up and reached for the book in his breast pocket which he felt had the answer, but the sound of heavy footsteps stopped him.

"Captain!" Hank's voice called to Roberts.

Roberts rose to his feet, then pulled himself up to the pier as he turned around to meet with Hank. His first mate was jogging towards him down the pier and waving.

"Did you find them?" Roberts asked when Hank came close.

"Aye, we did," Hank replied. "We found Kennedy and his cohorts drinking together at an inn not far from here. I had some of Edward's men who joined him not long ago secure a table to listen in and see if they can glean some information on where they may be heading next. Were you able to find their ships?"

Roberts nodded and pointed over to the row of ships. "The smallest on the right is Kennedy's, and I have no doubt that the other two are his companions."

"Thatch isn't due to arrive for another day, weather permitting. If they plan to leave on the morrow, then we must delay one of those ship's departure. We cannot fight all three ships, even with Thatch's help."

Roberts glanced around, wondering just how they would go about delaying a ship without drawing unwanted attention. After a moment of not-so-helpful ideas floating in his head, Roberts turned back around to Hank.

"We must first find out if they plan to set out tomorrow or not, and where. If they are to leave, we'll figure out something."

Roberts motioned for the other men to join them, then they followed Hank to the inn where Kennedy and his companions were staying. Hank led them to the back entrance of a small three-storey building close to the middle of the pier.

They entered the building through the server's entrance, and though there were men and women who worked at the inn they paid the pirates no heed. They were too busy to mind them, and chose to continue their work instead.

Hank walked casually through a hallway to the main hall and held the door open as he leaned over the threshold. "Kennedy and friends are at a table over in the corner there," Hank said, his eyes pointing where his hand dare not.

Roberts stepped forward and leaned inside as well. The main hall was bustling with activity, the tables and booths filled with patrons of all sorts. Merchants, sailors, and no doubt more pirates, were dining and drinking and telling stories in that room.

He followed Hank's eyes towards the corner of the other side of the room, and first noticed Edward's men sitting in a booth with drinks in hand, having a light conversation. Then, in the next seats over, he saw men he didn't recognize huddled together.

After a moment, the men pulled away from their huddle and got out of the booth they were sitting at. Then, Roberts saw the man they had been looking for, Walter Kennedy, standing there. Though his friend's face had changed a bit over the years—his cheeks shallow and his muscles more defined—there was no doubt it was the same Irishman he had worked with before.

Once more, Roberts felt the hot flash of anger rush

over him, and he found it difficult to control himself in the face of the man responsible. His feet moved of their own accord, but Hank's hand on Roberts' chest stopped him.

"They're coming this way," Hank said as he tried to push the massive Roberts back.

Roberts stepped back, and Hank pulled the door closed most of the way. Hank left a hair's breadth open so he could see through and watch their adversaries.

Roberts had to close his eyes, ball his fists, and take a few breaths to calm himself. He didn't know where this anger was coming from, and he was finding it difficult to cope with.

"They went upstairs to a room," Hank said over his shoulder. "Let's hope Edward's men were able to find something out. I'll go and fetch them."

Hank walked through the door, checked his sides, then went to retrieve the spies they had left. After a moment of talk, the men returned with Hank to the back of the inn.

"They say Kennedy and his associates got spooked and went to a room to finish discussing their plans. They were only able to find out that they do plan on leaving tomorrow, but not their heading."

Roberts was looking at the floor in silence as his companions stared at him.

"Bartholomew?" Hank called.

"I'm thinking," he replied, though in truth he was still trying to calm himself. After another moment, he looked up at Hank and the other crewmates. "We need to hear what's going on in that room... We might be able to watch them as they depart, but that doesn't mean they won't change course later. We may be after Kennedy, but

Edward is after the other crews. If things go south, we'll need to know where they're heading."

"What do we do then? We can't very well listen outside the door in full view of the inn's patrons, and there aren't any open balconies we could spy from."

Roberts took another moment to look in his men's eyes. "I'll need a drill... and a loud distraction."

Hank turned to Edward's men. "You'll be able to handle the distraction, won't you gents?" The men nodded and smiled in a way that spoke of their experience and joy in such matters. "Good. We'll give you a signal when we're ready." Hank pointed to one of their crewmates. "You find us a drill. There may be one in the stable out back. If not, ask the workers for one."

The crewmate turned to leave the inn in search of the drill, but Roberts stopped him. "We'll be in the room to the right of Kennedy, so bring the drill there." The crewmate gave an "Aye, Captain" before turning around again.

"Come, Hank, let's secure us a room." Roberts exited the hallway with Hank and the other crewmates following behind.

The five men from Edward's crew walked over to a table in the middle of the inn and joined a group playing a game with cards. Roberts went up the stairs to the second floor and kept a close watch on the door leading to Kennedy's room.

When they approached, Roberts took a quick glance at the room below, taking note of the inn staff. None were looking their way, so Roberts tapped on the door to the room they wanted to enter. If luck were on their side it would be empty, but the chances of that were unlikely.

It almost seemed as if luck was on their side, as there was no answer to Roberts' call. Roberts knocked on the door again, louder this time, and then came an answer.

"Hold, hold a moment," a man shouted from beyond the door.

After a few seconds, and a few grunting noises, Roberts heard footsteps coming to the door. The door opened, and a short and stocky man appeared before them. He wore a robe and nothing more, and his cheeks were red and his forehead slick with sweat.

"What in the Devil's name do you…" the man said, trailing off as his gaze shifted from the floor up Roberts' massive frame.

"We have need of your room for the moment, sir. If you'll excuse us," Roberts said.

Before the man could respond, Roberts placed his hand over the man's mouth and held fast to his cheeks. He pushed the man back into the room, and he and his crewmates entered.

In a bed near the back of the room, a woman was watching what was happening, and she let out a gasp as she sat up. Roberts bade her to quiet herself with a finger to his lips and a threatening look. She muffled a scream with her hands as tears formed in her eyes.

Hank closed the door behind them with a quick look towards the inn's first floor. "It doesn't appear as if we were seen," he said. "So far, so good."

Roberts pushed the man he was holding back to the bed next to the woman, and then leaned down to stare straight in his eyes. "Stay quiet, and nothing bad will happen to you. Understood?"

The man nodded as best he could, and Roberts released him with a small push causing him to fall on the bed. The woman came close to him and grabbed hold of his arm, the fear in both of their eyes telling Roberts that they would stay quiet.

Roberts looked at his crewmates. "Keep watch on them, and make sure we're not heard," he said. After his crew acknowledged the order, he went over to join Hank at the wall next to Kennedy's room.

Hank had his ear pressed up against the wall, his eyes closed, and his hands sprawled to his sides. Roberts joined his first mate in trying to listen through the wall, but he could only hear muffled voices and heavy boots smacking against the floor.

Before he could comment on the situation, there was a knock at the door. Roberts and Hank looked at each other, brows raised. Roberts removed himself from the wall and walked over to the door.

"Yes?" he called.

"Captain? I have the drill."

Roberts opened the door, glanced around the crewmate, and then pulled him in. The crewmate handed a small brace drill to Roberts.

"This will do nicely," Roberts said. He turned to Hank. "Hank, give the signal and keep watch for us."

Hank went to the door and opened it up wide. He stepped out, and then waved to give Edward's crewmates the signal. Hank came back in the room and left the door open a hair to see through.

Roberts moved to the other end of the wall, towards the back of the inn, and waited with the hand drill propped against the wood. He watched the door and Hank's back, his hands tensing on the curves of the brace handle and spindle.

After a moment's wait, Roberts could hear a rising commotion from beyond the door. It sounded as if a fight was breaking out downstairs, but it hadn't yet escalated beyond words. Another moment passed, and Roberts head a crash of glass, then shouting, and soon the whole inn erupted in noise.

Roberts had to give credit to Edward's men, as they knew how to make a ruckus. The first floor of the inn was already loud, and getting louder. Bottles and cups were thrown, chairs and tables broken, and all the while the shouts and fighting intensified. Some projectiles flew up to the second floor, knocking against the walls and doors of the inn's patrons.

Hank had to close the door shut for a moment as some of the debris was flung his way. Afterwards, he opened it up again and shifted his feet. He seemed to be looking at something. A moment passed, and Hank waved his hand in Roberts' direction without moving his focus from the opening in the door.

Roberts cranked the brace, moving the bit of the drill into the wood of the wall. With each turn of the brace, the bit dug into the grains of the wood. The noise of the inn overtook the noise of the wood breaking.

Roberts was already sweating, though not from the hard labour. He was a man of keen fitness, having been a sailor so long, and no small amount of drilling would tire him. His sweat came from the heat of the room, and the heat of stress. He kept splitting his focus from the drill and the wooden wall to his companion at the door, waiting for a signal to stop.

Roberts' hand slipped as the bit surged through the wall. The brace knocked against the wood with a loud thump, which caused all in the room, including Hank, to turn his way.

Roberts flashed his gaze over to Hank, and his horrified expression said everything. That thump was loud enough to be heard over the noise of the inn. He turned back to the drill and yanked it out of the wall, adding a scraping sound to the mix. He shook his head as his face washed over with rage over his blunders. He set the drill down on the floor and rushed to the bed with the room's occupants still sitting atop it.

"Make some noises as if you're having relations!" he said in a haste.

The man looked him up and down as if he were mad. "I shall do no su—"

Roberts directed his best vision of anger towards the two and said "Now!"

The tone and force of Roberts' words visibly shook the man, and he flashed his companion a flustered glance before he made some strained noises. His lover also joined in, and the two began making uneasy noises one might make during copulation—or at that point they could have been imitating goats, Roberts was unsure. After a moment, the two seemed to find their rhythm and it sounded more akin to the act than acting.

Roberts waved to his men, and they took hold of the bedframe. Following Roberts' lead, they rocked the bed back and forth with the couple's noises, ensuring it smacked against the wall a few times and scraped the floor some. The whole affair gave the appearance of some enthusiastic, though peculiar, love-making, which Roberts' hoped would cover for the noise made by the drill.

Roberts looked at Hank, and after a moment he closed the door, then went over to the hole Roberts had made. Hank took a look into the room and then listened through the hole, before waving to Roberts.

Roberts guided the couple and his crew into a crescendo finale before slowing the bed and the noise to a gradual finish, and then joined Hank.

Hank periodically switched from listening to peering through the hole in the wall. After a moment, he leaned over and whispered to Roberts.

"They're none the wiser about the hole. They seem to be discussing the noise."

Hank pressed his ear up against the wall once more and closed his eyes. Minutes passed with him listening intently to the conversation beyond the wall. He gave nary a clue of the goings on beyond a few shakes of his head. After the noise outside died down, and some more waiting, Hank's eyes shot open and he held his hand up.

Roberts waited on baited breath for Hank to say something, to tell them the news they so desperately wanted to hear. Hank's mouth was half open, the words on the tip of his tongue, and clear anticipation in his eyes. He too wanted to tell of what he was hearing, but didn't want to miss a detail.

"They leave on the morrow, as Edward's men said," Hank relayed in a whisper, his ear still pressed against the wood. "They head west until out of sight of the island, where they wait for their mark, a ship they plan to attack, at sunset." Hank listened for another minute before pulling himself away from the wall. "Now we have what we need. We can attack them with Edward and finally have our vengeance."

The other men in the room uttered slight hoots and chuckles, their fists clenched and smiles all around. Roberts once more thought on the word Hank used, and just what they were here to accomplish. Before he could ponder on what he was going to do with Walter Kennedy, Hank spoke again.

"So… have you thought about how we will delay one of their ships?"

In truth, Roberts hadn't had the chance, but when he looked at the hole beyond Hank's head, and the drill now lying on the floor, an idea formed.

"I'm of the mind that Kennedy's ship could use some modifications," he said as he picked up the drill.

3. A PERSONAL DECISION

From the Journal of Bartholomew Roberts
Entry #59 Dated July 10th, No Year Given

The weight of sin is heavy on my heart as of late.

I must make a decision which I have avoided for years, and I know not what I should do.

I sensed an anger well inside me which I did not know I possessed upon seeing Walter Kennedy. That anger calls for his head, but I know in my heart, and from the scriptures, that no good can come from anger.

I am a conflicted and contradictory man in many ways, and this decision serves now as a symbol of those contradictions.

I sin, yet I think I am fit to carry out justice. I am fallible, yet I think I am fit to judge others. I have anger in my heart, yet I seek so-called righteousness.

I am reminded of Luke's words of caution when trying to remove a speck from another's eye when there is a beam in one's own.

How can I say I am doing the work of God when I cannot tell if I have a beam affixed to my own eye?

Roberts and others on the *Fortune* watched the three ships owned by their enemies through the magnifying lenses of spyglasses. They kept a close eye on them as they prepared their ships to sail by the light of the morning sun.

The clear rays of light burst forward from across the horizon, affording Roberts a clear view of the three ships. He watched as the crews prepared their ships to leave, but paid special attention to the *Gallant*, the ship owned by Walter Kennedy.

Roberts and crew had been watching since the Gallant's initial preparations, and they were close to setting sail with nary a notion that anything was the matter with their ship. But Roberts noticed two crewmates rush up from below deck. They went straight to Kennedy, explained something to him, and then the three went back into the bowels of the ship.

"It appears they've found the holes we left for them," Hank said as he pulled away his own spyglass and looked over at Roberts.

"Now, all that's left is for the other ships to separate from the *Gallant* while they are stuck with repairs."

"Just as long as Kennedy doesn't suspect foul-play, we should be well to do."

"If luck is with us, they'll mistake the holes we left for wormrot."

Hank grinned. "Well, Captain, if there's one thing I've

learned about you, it's that you're the luckiest bastard to sail the seven seas."

Roberts and Hank both had a good chuckle, a rare event as of late, and it reminded him of their former captain, Howell Davis. Davis was a man of good humour but decisive action, and Roberts admired him. The thought brought with it a twinge of melancholy to the laughter, the kind only nostalgia and loss can bring.

Roberts pushed away the sad thoughts and peered through the small looking-glass once more to take in the view of the small sloop. It had two decent-sized masts, a hearty-looking crew, and planks not the worse for wear. From what Roberts could tell, the ship was fair to new, which meant Kennedy might not have been its captain for long.

"Tell me, Hank, do you recognize any aboard the Gallant?" Roberts asked.

Hank cast a brief sidelong glance at Roberts with his brow raised, then returned his attention to his spyglass. He stepped forward, closer to the ship railing, to see if he could get a better view. He moved his spyglass around, covering the *Gallant* from stem to stern.

"Strange," Hank muttered. "I fail to recognize any of the men working on that ship, save Kennedy from earlier of course."

"It seems our old friend has lost some company along the way," Roberts commented, leaning against the *Fortune's* railing.

Hank chuckled. "I reckon his leadership came into question."

"Perhaps," Roberts replied.

He stared at the planks of the sole, recalling the times when both he and Kennedy and Hank had shared the same space. Though at times exasperating, Roberts felt a kinship towards Kennedy. It was that kinship which made Roberts nostalgic in that moment, but it also helped him understand exactly why the betrayal had stung so much over time.

The sound of Hank shuffling brought Roberts' attention back, and he looked up to see Hank peering at the *Gallant* through his spyglass again. Roberts turned around and did the same, and he could see Kennedy back on the top deck again.

Kennedy went over to the side of the ship where his companion's ships were floating. He had one hand cupped over his mouth, and he was shouting something over the side at them. Soon, the men in the other pirate ship listened to what he was saying, and presumably their captain was conversing with him.

The conversation went on for a few moments, and the other captain appeared vexed by Kennedy. He left the conversation with a huff and a wave of his hands. Kennedy's crew stared at him as his hand dropped to his side. He turned around and seemed startled at the men gathered around him. After a moment, he too waved them away with a word, and then went back below deck.

After a few moments, the two larger sloops let loose their sails and headed off to the west, just as they had overheard. They left the *Gallant* behind too, just as they had hoped.

Roberts lips curled into a sly smile as he turned to look at Hank, who was also smiling. "Men!" Roberts called as he faced the crew. "I want this ship ready to sail at a moment's notice. We need to follow that sloop out to sea, where we can take the battle to her without fear of interruption from the Providencia locals. We'll have need of all our speed in the coming battle, and you'll need to keep your wits about you if we're to succeed… though I understand wits may be hard for some of you to come by," he said with a jovial chuckle, which the crew reciprocated.

As the men prepared the ship, Roberts walked off towards the bow cabin. "Hank, I'm going to take a moment of rest in the cabin. Inform me when the *Gallant* begins to move, would you?"

"Aye, Captain," he replied behind Roberts.

Bartholomew Roberts left the crew to their task, and entered the small cabin at the front of the ship. He almost had to bend over to walk around, but it was his most favourite spot aboard the *Fortune*. He found its viewing windows out to the bow pleasant for contemplation, and there was a large table on which he could dine should he choose to. And, whether he wanted company or simply a moment of reprieve, it never felt too empty or too crowded. It was the perfect size, even if it took a bend of the knee to traverse.

Roberts went to the far side of the cabin, turned a chair around, and leaned back in it as he watched the goings on in Providencia. The sun had risen above the horizon to Roberts right. Though he couldn't see the sun itself, its brilliance shone against the buildings and shadows cast away from it.

Sailors in various combinations of cotton and wool cloth greeted each other as they prepared to sell the last of their cargo before sailing off. Men and women and children all began their morning routines, walking this way and that, not aware that soon, just off their shores, pirates would be battling each other.

As Roberts watched the people going about their business, the fatigue and tiredness that had built up over his lack of sleep struck him, and he let out a great yawn. His eyes grew heavy, and he had trouble keeping them open. As it usually happens, before he could take notice, he was falling asleep.

⚓ ⚓ ⚓

Roberts awoke with a start as his chair slammed on the planks of the cabin. He took a deep breath in through his nose and flashed his gaze to the left and right of him to gather his bearings. He soon remembered where he was, and his senses came rushing back to him.

His gaze soon settled upon the bow of the ship once more, and he noticed that not much had changed since the time of his sleep other than the light on the pier and town.

The startling awakening had jolted him and caused a stir in his heart, which now beat loudly in his chest. As he calmed himself, he once more remembered what he was waiting for, and his thoughts turned to his decision.

He knew what the book in his pocket would say, and he felt the itch to pull it out for the guidance it always provided him, but at the same time he wanted to leave it where it was. He wanted to keep his anger for Kennedy, and work the same justice his friend, Edward Thatch, spoke of.

The door opened, startling Roberts. He rose to his feet and turned around to see Hank leaning in through the doorway. "The *Gallant* is readying their sails, Captain," he said.

Roberts nodded, and Hank nodded back before starting to leave and close the door. "Hank," Roberts called. "A moment… please?"

Hank turned back around, a strange look in his eyes, and entered the cabin, closing the door behind him. "Yes,

Captain?"

Roberts turned his seat around towards the table and waited until Hank was seated. "I…" he began, but he didn't know what to say. He leaned forward and looked away from Hank's gaze for a moment, searching for the right words. "I need your help," he said finally.

Hank leaned back in his chair. "It's about Kennedy, isn't it?"

Roberts replied with a curt nod of the head, but he didn't look Hank in the eyes. "I… I know not what I should do. I fear that time and anger has clouded my judgement, and I am in need of guidance." Even Roberts could hear the pleading in his own voice. He thought himself pathetic, but when he looked up at his first mate, Hank, he had a smile on his face. "You think I am jesting?"

Hank shook his head. "No—no, of course not," he said profusely. "I know that when the time comes you'll know what to do. You always do."

Roberts couldn't help but cock his brow and sit up in his chair. "But… what of the crew? They have a say in this decision as well, and they seem to be calling for Kennedy's blood."

Hank waved his hand as though he were waving away smoke. "The crew will respect your decision on the matter. Kennedy was your friend first and foremost, and you are the captain. You have the right and authority to make this decision."

Roberts let out a sigh and leaned back in his chair. "But what if I make the wrong decision?"

Hank stared at Roberts for a moment, and then he got up from his chair. He walked over to a cabinet at the side of the cabin and pulled out a bottle of whiskey. He poured some of the drink into two glasses, then handed one to

Roberts.

"Drink," he commanded. Roberts downed the alcohol in one great gulp, barely letting the taste of it touch his tongue. Hank did the same, and then placed the cup on the table. "Trust in yourself," he said, standing tall above the sitting Roberts. "It's brought you this far, hasn't it?"

Hank didn't wait for Roberts to give him an answer, instead electing to leave the cabin and prepare the ship with the other crewmates.

Roberts waited for a moment, his empty cup still in hand, thinking on what his first mate had said. He placed the cup on the table next to Hank's, rose from his seat, and left the cabin.

The sun hit his eyes and forced his hand up to cover the blinding rays. He looked over towards the source, and saw the *Gallant* and her crew preparing to leave once more. The men on the weather deck were unlashing the sails, readying them for the orders to drop the canvas.

When Roberts turned his attention back to his own crew, he noticed several of the men looking at him. He could see the anticipation in their eyes, the tension in their clenched fists and force building in their legs. They were waiting for him to make the call. Even though they too were ready to drop the sails and head out for battle, they wanted him to direct their built-up energy from two years gone by.

"Alright men, let's capture us a sloop!" Roberts shouted.

The men responded with a loud chorus of cheers and hoots. The energy and tension surged from them in an instant, and the roar of their fervour filled the ship and spilled out like a great wave from a mighty storm. Soon, they would direct that storm at the *Gallant*, and there would be no escape for her. Of that, Roberts was sure.

Bartholomew Roberts' Justice

After the revelry died down, they took the *Fortune* out of the harbour and into the sea. They sailed away from the island of Providencia and to the west. The *Gallant* was not long to join them in their wake.

As the *Fortune* bounced and jumped with the waves, the wind whipping against the sails and sending spray across the deck, Roberts held fast to the starboard railing at the stern. He kept an eye pressed into his spyglass and watched as the *Gallant* crept up behind them.

Roberts turned around and moved midship. "Keep the name of our ship covered. We don't want to spook Kennedy before we have the chance to strike."

Several crew members stood watch on the side of the ship already covered by spare sail canvas. They kept their feet on the loose parts, and their eyes pinned below to ensure it stayed in place.

As the minutes turned to hours, the two ships left sight of Providencia, holding steady to the western direction. The *Gallant*, being the smaller of the two, had the advantage in speed, and advanced on the *Fortune* as the time passed. The *Gallant* gave Roberts' ship a wide berth, but were they lined up they would be touching stern to stem. At around high noon they reached the edge of what the people of Providencia could see and hear from sea.

"Two points to port! Prepare broadside!" Roberts shouted. "Show them who we are."

His men returned the order with a loud "Aye!" before heading to task. The helmsman spun the wheel, and the ship shifted to the left towards the *Gallant* in a South South-West direction. At the same time, the men prepared muskets under the cover of the masts.

The men covering the name of the ship with canvas removed the loose sail to show their name, and those in the crow's nest let loose their Jolly Roger. The black flag showed Roberts holding an hourglass next to death itself, and was a fearsome warning to all who saw it that their time was running out. Roberts hoped that Kennedy could see and understand the meaning of that flag.

As if in answer to Roberts' call to battle, clouds rushed in overhead and blocked the sun from view. The warm rays no longer shone on their actions, and instead brought a cold air with it.

Though Roberts felt the chill, he paid it no heed. He was too focused on the fight to come, too focused on the enemy in front of him to notice the lost light above him.

"Fire!" Roberts called.

His men answered with the sound of cannons erupting from below deck. The wave of iron burst from their shells and cascaded upon the wooden ship to port. The sound of the iron crashing against the wood, splintering and shattering the planks to pieces, returned as music to Roberts' ears.

The unprovoked attack caught the crew of the *Gallant* wholly unawares, but they hastily turned the ship southwest as well. After a few minutes, the *Gallant* returned fire with her swivel guns at the stern before giving a lacklustre broadside off the starboard bow.

Fortune sustained only light damage on the port bow, as most of the shots ended up in the drink between the ships. The crew were unharmed, save perhaps a splinter or two from broken planks.

The crew of the *Fortune* returned fire with their own swivel guns along the bow, but the *Gallant's* speed advantage was widening the gap between the two ships.

"We should turn to port and rake their stern, otherwise they're liable to do the same to our bow, Captain," Hank said.

Bartholomew Roberts' Justice

Roberts shook his head. "No, we can't do that. We can't risk losing that ship."

Hank looked from Roberts to the *Gallant* and back, and he clenched his teeth. He stepped forward, closer to Roberts. "Captain, if this is what you want, then I stand by it, but you have to face the fact that they're about to sail away. If Kennedy runs, we may never find him again."

Roberts glanced at Hank only briefly, but it was all he needed to see the urgency in his eyes. Roberts looked at the shrinking stern of the *Gallant* as splashes of water from cannonballs shot up in the air between the two ships.

His hand tightened into a ball. "Hard to port! Load starboard cannons for raking fire!" he shouted.

Before anyone could move to carry out Roberts' orders, a man on the weather deck shouted "Ship closing in from the south!" and pointed off the port side of the ship.

Roberts looked over at the crewmate who shouted, and followed his finger to see the ship that was approaching. They had been too preoccupied with the battle to notice the ship coming in, and it was already closing in on the two sloops.

As Roberts took note of the ship in question, he couldn't help but smile. "Belay that order!" he shouted to the helmsman. "Keep us steady and give us all the speed you can."

Hank was beside Roberts, and he too was looking at the approaching ship, but from the look on his face he didn't understand Roberts' reaction. "What do you see, Captain?"

"That's the *Queen Anne's Revenge*, I have no doubt of it."

Hank glanced at Roberts, then back at the ship coming their way. He nodded. "You may be correct. It has three masts, and by its size I reckon it is a frigate. What do you propose we do?"

Roberts thought it over a moment. "Hmm... We steady our course, head west so they can't tack north, and hope the *Queen Anne's Revenge* cuts them off from the south." Roberts glanced around at the sails and the way they flapped in the wind. "With the wind as it is, our companions have the advantage and should send the *Gallant* running."

Hank smiled and let out a brief chuckle as he shook his head.

"What?" Roberts asked, a smile tugging at the corner of his mouth as well.

"Your luck knows no bounds, Captain. That Thatch would appear now of all times; none would have taken that bet."

"Perhaps it's luck, or perhaps we have someone watching over us," Roberts replied.

"Perhaps," Hank concurred.

Roberts told the helmsman to turn them back to the west and slightly away from the *Gallant*. As the ship changed course, the mood aboard also seemed to shift, or it could have just been Roberts' perception that had changed. No longer a desperate struggle with thoughts of Kennedy escaping once more, now it was a true chase against a prey they knew they would best.

Over the next thirty minutes, the three ships stayed their courses, with the *Queen Anne's Revenge* closing in on the *Gallant*. When they were close, Edward's ship fired a few shots from their cannons, though they fell well short of the *Gallant* and served as a simple warning. The *Gallant* took the warning, and whether it was from Kennedy's bumbling or the crew's inexperience, they seemed to forget about the *Fortune*. They almost tacked into the wind towards the *Fortune*, but turned back before it was too late.

The damage was done, and they lost what little advantage in speed they had from the manoeuvre.

The *Gallant* furled their sails, and a man came up to the stern to wave a white flag of surrender. They won the battle, with no major injuries or casualties either.

"Furl the sails! Bring us next to the *Gallant*!"

The crew did as commanded and raised the sails, putting them away and leaving the *Fortune* with the current. The helmsman twisted the wheel and the two ships came closer and closer.

All the while, Edward's ship was closing in not far behind them, though slower than the other two ships.

"Stay armed, men. We don't know yet if they plan to ambush us," Hank warned.

The *Fortune* glided up next to the *Gallant* and the crew were quick to lash the boats together and drop gangplanks across the side. Afterwards, Roberts and his men boarded the enemy ship with their weapons drawn and ready to fire.

Roberts' pirates pointed each musket and cutlass they had at the enemy crew, and the look in their eyes called to the itch they felt at the trigger and handle of their weapons. There was no denying that they wanted a fight, and they were just waiting for an opportunity to strike.

The *Gallant's* crew were not going to give them that opportunity, however, as they seemed eager to yield to Roberts' crew. They willingly moved to the centre of the ship, some with their hands raised in submission, and offered no resistance.

Roberts searched the crowd of people waiting in the middle of the ship. Some men were wounded from previous attacks, with fresh or dried blood covering their faces, heads, or other extremities. There didn't seem to be any dead from what Roberts could see, but the ship had suffered minor damage from the barrage of cannons.

"Where is your captain?" Roberts questioned in an angry tone. "Where is Walter Kennedy?" he said, his melodic Welsh accent taking on a harsh tone that frightened the *Gallant's* crew. If not his accent, then his stature alone inspired the fear he saw in their eyes. Despite the fear, none answered his call. Roberts turned to a few of his crewmates. "Find him," he said.

Two crewmates left and went below deck in search of Walter Kennedy. Hank walked over to Roberts, glancing at the crew and the ship as he approached.

"The ship doesn't appear to be too badly damaged," he said.

Roberts nodded, taking another look at the ship. "Aye, it should sail nicely." He looked at the men in the centre of the ship, those who had surrendered. "It's as we thought, Kennedy's crew is his own… I see no familiar faces."

Hank folded his arms in front of his chest. "And not a one of them's got so much as a rind on them. They're all as green as a summer field."

Roberts took note of the age of those in Kennedy's crew; they couldn't be much past their teens, if that. A few were older, perhaps old enough to have worked on a ship before, but they looked to have neither the experience nor the fortitude to work as a pirate.

As Roberts was looking over the crew, the large frigate of his ally, Edward Thatch, the young Blackbeard, was setting up next to the *Gallant*. His crew dropped a gangplank across the gap, and Edward walked over.

Edward was tall, nearly as tall as Roberts, and well built. He carried himself with a fearsome countenance that had grown since the two had met years prior when Roberts was hot on Kennedy's trail. His deathly stare and great black beard were enough to make most men cower, but from their time together Roberts knew that beneath that gaze lay a man solely devoted to his crew whom he considered family.

"Roberts, I'm glad we made it in time," Edward said.

Roberts shook Edward's hand. "Well met, Edward. I too am glad you arrived when you did. It could have been a long, arduous endeavour without your assistance." Roberts glanced at the Queen Anne's Revenge. "I see you've completed your modifications to the ship. It looks like a whole new vessel."

Edward glanced over his shoulder at his ship. "Aye, she's faster now as well. We might even be able to challenge you," he said.

Roberts flashed a slight grin, but said nothing. Before Edward could say anything else, Roberts' crewmates returned to the weather deck.

His crew carried with him Walter Kennedy, and prodded him forward with muskets at his back. Kennedy was already cowering in fear at the sight of his former crew and captain. His back was arched with a hunch, and sweat covered his face. The crew pushed him in front of Roberts and Edward, and he fell to his knees.

The sight of Kennedy once again brought anger into Roberts' heart, and his face felt flush. His hands and teeth were clenched as he forced himself to hold back from attacking the man right then and there.

Edward cocked and primed a pistol, then turned it over to Roberts. "Time for justice, Roberts."

Roberts looked at the pistol in his hands for a moment, and then pointed it at Kennedy. Kennedy's eyes were filled with fear and despair. "Please, Roberts," he said with a trembling voice. "I—"

"Shut your mouth, Walter," Roberts seethed as he took a step forward and pressed the pistol against Kennedy's forehead.

Kennedy sobbed and closed his eyes, letting out a pathetic cry like a mewling babe. His whole body shook, and it looked as if at any moment he might soil himself. His hands clasped together in front of him, tightening in preparation for what was about to happen.

Roberts' finger was on the trigger, ready to fire. His anger was intense and overwhelming as he thought back to all the times Kennedy had wronged him, or even simply annoyed him.

Then, just as Roberts was about to pull the trigger, the clouds above parted, letting the light through to shine on the three ships. Roberts hesitated, and in that hesitation the seeds of doubt spread. He remembered words that he wanted to ignore, but couldn't in that moment. Words from the bible.

'Be angry, but sin not: let not the sun go down upon your wrath.' 'The discretion of man deferreth his anger: and his glory is to pass by an offence.' 'For the wrath of man doth not accomplish the righteousness of God.'

"Roberts," Edward said, a nervous chuckle following his call, "what are you doing?"

Roberts sighed, but then smiled. "You are correct. Now is the time for justice, Edward. My justice." He looked at Walter Kennedy. "I will grant you mercy this day, old friend. You will live to see another day."

4. MATTHEW 6:14

From the Journal of Bartholomew Roberts
Entry #60 Dated July 11th, No Year Given

I have lost many friends by my actions.

Edward couldn't accept that I would grant Walter mercy, and has left our company. The young man is becoming a pirate through and through. The kind of pirate whispered about to bring fear to the hearts of man. He has become hardened by the years, and that hardness has stripped him of all kindness.

And I do not blame him for his anger.

Though I have granted Walter mercy, the contradiction remains. Though forgiveness is on my lips, it has not reached my heart.

I do not regret what I have done, and yet I do all the same. My mind is as two sides of a coin, being tossed in the air and caught just to see what side I land on in that moment.

My crew has accepted my decision, though I know some, like Edward, do not understand why I chose to do what I did.

In truth, I feel it was only that the coin landed on the side it was meant to at that time.

A knock came at Roberts' cabin door. "Enter," he beckoned.

Hank opened the door and walked inside the cabin. "Captain... a word?"

Roberts nodded and motioned for Hank to take a seat at his table. Roberts had been writing in his journal, and as Hank approached he dried and set the quill down, then placed a stopper in the ink bottle.

"What is it you wish to talk of, Hank?"

Before Hank sat down, he took another bottle of alcohol from the cabinet and filled two glasses. "I thought we could have a drink, if it pleases you?"

Roberts closed the book of his journal and chuckled. "Lord knows I need a drink after all this."

Hank wore a wide grin as he turned around, glasses in hand. "Why do you think I offered?"

Roberts chuckled once again as Hank placed the glass in front of him. He took a drink, savouring the sweet notes of citrus on the back of the brandy as he sipped.

"How is the crew taking what's happened?"

"They're upset that we've lost allies, but they accept your judgement. Just as I said."

"Just as you said..." Roberts repeated.

As Roberts and Hank sipped on the brandy, they had a silent moment together. They could hear the lap of the waves against the ship, the stomp of feet against the roof of the cabin, and the general shouting customary aboard a ship.

The two relaxed in each other's company, enjoying the momentary reprieve from battle and difficult decisions. They had been through much over the years, and though these times were few and far between, Roberts appreciated them all the same.

"You know, it's quite the bit of magic you've done with this crew," Hank blurted out.

Roberts arched his brow and grinned. "Whatever do you mean?"

Hank leaned forward in his chair and held his glass in front of him as he looked off to the side. "I've been sailing for as long as I can remember. Sailed with some of the hardest men you would have ever met, and that was even before falling in with this pirating business…" Hank trailed off for a moment, and then took another drink of his brandy. "Davis, he… he uh, he was bright, but he never really had the kind of focus you have," he said, referring to their original captain. "It was always about the next score, the next place to plunder, and there wasn't much thought beyond that. The only reason he freed slaves was because some of the crew felt strongly about it. You though…" he said, pointing at Roberts, "you gave us rules, structure. You showed us that we could be better men than simple brutes. At first, I thought the men would revolt after so many rules, like with Kennedy, but they stuck by you. They might not always agree with you, but they stood by you just the same. I don't think I've ever seen someone who could inspire such loyalty." Hank took another drink of his brandy, and then chuckled. "I mean what kind of a person could convince a pirate crew to… to free slaves, give up prostitutes, and show mercy to our enemies?"

Roberts laughed along with his friend. "You flatter me, my friend. I do not think so great of myself, especially in this." He took a drink, then looked off to the side, just as Hank did when reminiscing. "I chastised the young Edward for his anger and acting on whims, when I too acted on a whim. I felt the anger in my heart against Kennedy, and I wanted to shoot him. I cast aside our greatest allies because I could not face my reflection in his eyes. I'm just a coward who ran away."

"Tch," Hank spat. "It takes more courage to forgive than to fight. Any man can pull a trigger in the hopes it fixes all their troubles. It takes true strength to know when to pull the trigger, and when to pull back."

Roberts had to look away from Hank's fierce eyes. He didn't feel worthy of all the praise, though he knew time would settle his mind. "Perhaps you are right," he said, trying to appease his friend.

Roberts downed the rest of the drink and rose from his chair. "I believe I should pay our temporary prisoner a visit. Keep the ship running for me, would you?"

Hank nodded and raised his glass as Roberts passed him by. Roberts left the cabin, closing the door behind him, and headed below deck. First, Roberts headed to the galley and grabbed some dry biscuits, and then headed to the makeshift brig; a cargo room with some of the crew keeping watch both inside and out.

Roberts greeted his men before entering the cargo room, and searched the faces of the men sequestered there. Off in one corner he noticed Walter Kennedy sitting on a barrel with his back against the wall. Roberts went over to Kennedy, and pulled over a box to sit on next to him.

Bartholomew Roberts' Justice

Roberts slapped Kennedy's leg and he woke with a start. When his eyes met Roberts' they widened in shock and he straightened himself. "John! I… I'm sorry, I'd not seen ye there," he said, his Irish accent breaking through, unchanged after so many years.

Roberts smiled as he broke off a piece of a biscuit and handed it to Kennedy. "It's Bartholomew now, remember?"

Kennedy nodded, embarrassment clear on his face, as he took the biscuit. "Aye, of course… From that ni—I mean… from yer former slave friend who passed."

Roberts took a bite from his half of the biscuit. "Yes, I took his name as my own," he said. "That was… quite some time ago, wasn't it?"

Kennedy grinned. "Aye, an age and a half."

The sounds of the ship were amplified in those small quarters, with the sound of the other prisoners' whispers heard above all else. Silence took over the space between the two old friends, and the air felt thick with tension.

Roberts couldn't help but feel a strangeness in the pit of his stomach. His eyes flitted between the hull of his ship and the biscuit in his hand as he thought of what to say. What does one say to someone who betrayed you, who you're still angry with, and who you're trying to forgive?

"So…" Kennedy started, cutting the tension. "What did ye end up using all them jewels ye stole fer?" he said with a grin.

Roberts looked up at Kennedy and arched his brow. "Jewels?"

"Aye, the jewels ye stole from the King o' Portugal. I heard that ye succeeded, 'less that was some other bloke with the name Bartholomew Roberts what stole some

King's jewels," Kennedy said with a laugh.

Roberts joined in the laughter and nodded his head as he remembered that night. The night that Kennedy absconded with his other ship. "We lived like Kings... though modest ones, and it's brought us this far. Some of the coin made its way to parishes here and there, or others who needed it more than I or the crew."

"Sounds like your doing," Kennedy commented. He looked over Roberts' shoulder at the crewmates standing guard at the door. "I see many a familiar face 'ere. Still with all the same men?"

Roberts glanced over his shoulder to see who Kennedy was looking at. "Aye. Some men come and go, as is the case, but we're mostly unchanged."

"That's good," Kennedy said, leaning his head back against the hull while looking down at his feet as he took the last bite of his biscuit.

Roberts handed Kennedy another. "What happened to the *Royal Rover* and her crew?"

Kennedy lost his smile and kept staring at his feet. "We left that night high on the thought that we had made the right choice. We learned of yer success later, and it became a bitter victory," he said, taking another bite of the dry cracker. "We struggled ta find ships with cargo worth attacking, and with each ship we brought down we barely had enough ta feed ourselves. Before our mutiny I sold myself as captain by saying I knew how ta navigate. When the men found it to be a lie, they left me at the next port and set off on their own."

Roberts could hear the frustration and sadness in Kennedy's voice, but he bade him to continue the story. "What did you do after that?"

Kennedy looked up at Roberts for a moment, then returned his gaze to his feet. "Went from port to port, picked up a few things on navigating, and found me a part of a growing pirate crew. They gave me a ship ta command, and I named it the *Gallant* as ye saw. They gave me the worst ship, with the greenest lot you'd ever seen, but I didn't care; I had a ship to call my own. Would'a ran away from 'em eventually, but ye found me, and here we are."

"And here we are…" Roberts echoed.

There was another brief moment of silence before Kennedy once again broke it. "Did ye patch things up with yer friend?"

"Edward?" Roberts asked. Kennedy nodded. "No," Roberts replied as he shook his head. "The boy couldn't accept that I would show you mercy, and we've parted ways."

Kennedy's mouth made a line, and he said, "I'm sorry," as he looked away.

"It would have occurred regardless, I feel."

Kennedy was shaking his head as he looked off to the other side of the ship. "I've caused ye such trouble over the years... Caused so many people trouble…"

Roberts smacked Kennedy on the leg. "All is forgiven, no need to wallow any more," he said.

"I'm… I'm nothing but a coward. I don't deserve your forgiveness," he said. Before Roberts could say something else, Kennedy continued. "I need to tell you something… something I did back when Davis was still our captain."

Roberts sat up and eyed Kennedy. "Go on."

"When we were on that island, just before he died… I… I ran away," Kennedy said. There was a pause, and Kennedy looked at Roberts for a response. When he didn't receive one he continued. "I was there with 'im. I could'a fought, and, who knows, we may have survived together. But I was a coward, and I ran," Kennedy held his hands up to his head. "Oh, God... Roberts, I left 'im ta die out there," he said, his voice trembling and tears dripping from his eyes.

Roberts was stunned, not by the revelation, but by the confession. To see Kennedy reduced to tears in front of him caused him to feel pangs of sadness for his old friend. The years did not seem to have been kind to him, but he hadn't the fortitude to carry on in guilt. To be able to confess to Roberts must have been like a weight lifting off him.

Roberts placed his hand on Kennedy's shoulder. "And yet, by doing as you did, you were able to save countless lives aboard the *Royal Rover*," he said. "I forgive you, Walter, for all that you've done. Whether in secret or not, I forgive you."

Kennedy fell off his seat and to his knees on the sole of the ship. Roberts went with him, and held fast to his hands as the man wept. His tears hit the wooden floorboards and disappeared into the ether as his sins were forgiven.

Roberts said a silent prayer for his old friend and crewmate, in the hopes that he would lead a happy life from then on.

⚓ ⚓ ⚓

The *Fortune* landed in Providencia just before nightfall, where they let the former crew of the *Gallant* go. Thankfully, the crew were cooperative and gave Roberts' crew no issues as they left in longboats to shore.

Kennedy stood at the edge of the *Fortune's* starboard

side, getting ready to enter the last longboat with a pack of simple supplies slung over his shoulder. Roberts was there with him, and the two looked over towards the town as men and women milled about before heading home for the night.

"Well, I suppose this is goodbye, ain't it?" Kennedy said.

"Yes, I suppose so," Roberts replied, extending his hand.

Kennedy took Roberts' hand and gave it a firm shake before returning his attention to the longboat and shore. After a moment, he leaned over to Roberts. "Ye wouldn't be looking for an extra deckhand, would ye?" he said with a chuckle.

Roberts laughed as well. "No, I should like to keep my ship this time." He smacked Kennedy on the back and pushed him forward towards the longboat. "Safe travels, Walter."

Kennedy glanced over his shoulder and said, "The same to ye, Bartholomew."

Walter Kennedy boarded the longboat, and he was taken to the shore of Providencia with the last of his crew. Afterwards, the crew of the *Fortune* brought the longboats back, and they were promptly secured to the ship once more.

Hank came up beside Roberts. "What now, Captain?"

Roberts gave Hank a sidelong glance. "Now? Now, we set off for our next adventure!" he said with a grin.

Hank smiled, scratched his chin, and took a few steps forward. "Alright you lazy sods, the night's not over for you yet. Get this ship under way!" he shouted, and the crew replied with a booming "Aye, Aye!" in return.

The sails were set, the ship turned around, and they

headed off away from the island. As the ship began moving, Roberts went to the stern and looked at the receding island. He noticed Walter standing on the pier, watching them depart.

Roberts waved to Kennedy, and Kennedy waved back, signalling their final goodbye to one another, and the last time they would see each other alive.

⚓ ⚓ ⚓

Walter Kennedy settled in Ireland, giving up on his dreams of pirating and being a captain to run a brothel. He was later accused of a theft he did not commit, and outed as a pirate by a former crewmate in a bid for a reduced sentence. Walter was later tried for piracy, and hung at the gallows. His crewmate, never learning the true lesson of mercy given by Bartholomew Roberts as in Matthew 18: 21-35, was also tried and hung for piracy.

THE END

OTHER BOOKS
BY THE AUTHOR

The Pirate Priest Series:

BARTHOLOMEW ROBERTS' FAITH

BARTHOLOMEW ROBERTS' JUSTICE

BARTHOLOMEW ROBERTS' MERCY

BARTHOLOMEW ROBERTS' SPIRIT

The Voyages of Queen Anne's Revenge Series:

BLACKBEARD'S FREEDOM

BLACKBEARD'S REVENGE

BLACKBEARD'S JUSTICE

BLACKBEARD'S FAMILY

The Collection Series:

BLACKBEARD'S SHIP (Includes Books 1&2 of The Voyages of Queen Anne's Revenge & The Pirate Priest)

BLACKBEARD'S BLOOD (Includes Books 3&4 of The Voyages of Queen Anne's Revenge & The Pirate Priest)

ABOUT THE AUTHOR

JEREMY IS CURRENTLY LIVING IN NEW BRUNSWICK, CANADA WITH HIS WIFE HEATHER, AND THEIR TWO CATS, NAVI AND THOR.

Jeremy's first foray into the writing world was during a writing competition called NaNoWriMo, where the goal is to write a certain number of words in the month of November.

After completing the novel he started, and some extensive rewrites, he felt it was worthy of publishing and self-published his first novel, Blackbeard's Freedom in September, 2012.

After writing over ten books under two names, his passion for writing hasn't wavered over the years, and hopes to one day make it his primary career.

Let everyone know what you thought of his novels by leaving a review. He loves getting feedback on his books, and loves to hear from fans of his work.

Want to pirate one of Jeremy's audiobooks? Visit www.mcleansnovels.com/faith-audiobook-offer for a free copy of one of his audiobooks.